# Identity
## *You're Not Who You're Pretending to Be*

DARRIUS GETER

Copyright © 2017 Darrius Geter

All rights reserved.

ISBN:197941730X
ISBN-13: 978-1979417303

## DEDICATION

*To Taylor (Little Beautiful).*
*Because you weren't born for the first one.*

# CONTENTS

| | | |
|---|---|---|
| 1 | Who Are You? | 3 |
| 2 | The Power of Purpose | 9 |
| 3 | Identity & Purpose | 21 |
| 4 | Identity Influences Behavior | 35 |
| 5 | Negative Identity | 48 |
| 6 | Brokenness | 54 |
| 7 | Creating Your Own Identity | 62 |
| 8 | Questioning Your Worth | 76 |
| 9 | You Must Die | 84 |
| 10 | Deliver Me From My Issues | 98 |
| 11 | Leaving the Known for the Unknown | 112 |
| 12 | Stretched to the Next Level | 122 |
| 13 | Where Is Your Vision | 128 |
| 14 | Call Forth Your Potential | 136 |
| 15 | Success Embedded Within Us | 146 |
| 16 | Discovering Your Identity | 162 |

# IDENTITY

# Chapter 1

## WHO ARE YOU?

*"One day the evil spirit answered them, Jesus I know, and Paul I know about, but who are you?"*

- Acts 19:15

Who am I? People have spent their entire lives searching for the answer to that question. Many of the issues we face in life can be attributed to the notion that we do not know who we are. Low self-esteem, lack of self-confidence, lack of self-respect, and other self-related issues can be attributed to lacking the knowledge of our own identity.

When we do not know our identity, we force ourselves to settle for less than we are entitled to have from the promises of God. Rather than living a life with dominion authority as the Word of God promises, we become subject to our domain; living an oppressed life, beaten down by the very forces God has given us the power to take authority over.

In the scripture (*See Acts 19:11-16*), the Bible tells us God was performing marvelous miracles through the Apostle Paul. The anointing on Paul was so powerful that even the handkerchiefs that he'd touched healed sicknesses and caused evil spirit to flee. Because of the popularity that Paul had obtain by preaching and performing miracles in the name of Jesus, the sons of a Jewish chief priest started casting out demons *"in the name of Jesus whom Paul preaches."*

Because these men did not know Jesus personally, they had an encounter with a demonically oppressed man who overpowered and beat them severely.

What these verses of scripture tell us is that when we do not know our identity, we imitate those who do. They exude a self confidence that is attractive to us. Because we desire to be as confident within ourselves as those we imitate, we place ourselves in situations and circumstances that we cannot handle or should not be in because we are attempting to be someone we are not.

Ask yourself, how many times have you done things, bought things, went places, and interacted with people you really should not have simply because you were trying to maintain an image or identity that was not truly you?

Had the sons of Sceva discovered their identity through Jesus rather than only knowing Jesus through the Apostle Paul, not only would they have been secured in who they were personally without the need to imitate someone else, but they would not have been humiliated and beaten by an evil spirit that through God they would have had authority over.

## *Our Identity*

Our identity is uniquely our own, it cannot be duplicated by anyone else. As such, we cannot duplicate the identity of anyone else and expect to live a fulfilling life. Just like no two snowflakes are alike and no two finger prints are alike, God did not create two people to have the same identity. Because our identity is unique to us, the purpose for our lives is unique to us and cannot be fulfilled by anyone else.

We may think we know who we are, and we may even choose to identify ourselves according to our own standards and beliefs. However, identity can only be found in God. It is only when we come to our creator, confessing Jesus as our Lord and Savior; laying down our lives for Him that we can come to the knowledge of who we really are. Once we know who we are in Jesus, we know the purpose of our lives.

Knowing who we are in Jesus and the purpose for which God created us gives us our identity.

# Chapter 2

## THE POWER OF PURPOSE

*"The word of the Lord came to Jonah son of Amittai: Go to the great city of Nineveh and preach against it, because its wickedness has come up before me. But Jonah ran away from the Lord and headed for Tarshish…"*

- Jonah 1:1-3

There is nothing more important in life than having purpose. We could all stand to ask ourselves the question, why am I here? What did God put me on Earth for and am I doing it? Purpose is the reason that something exists. Not only is purpose the reason something exists, but we must understand that there is *power* in having *purpose*.

Purpose most times is taken for granted. The idea of how important and powerful it is to have a purpose in our lives does not really hit us until it is taken from us or we lose it. For instance, we will complain about having to get up Monday – Friday at four or five O'clock in the morning to get ready for work, fight traffic, and deal with people at work that get on our nerves.

We'll complain about how much work we must do with so little pay in return. But the moment our employer starts talking about downsizing, laying people off or cutting cost, there is a tenseness within us because we understand that the *purpose*; the reason behind us enduring so much aggravation daily is to earn a living to provide for our family.

It is only when our purpose is taken away from us that we realize how powerful having a purpose in our lives really is. It's not only important to understand the power that purpose has in our lives, but we must also understand that the purpose for our lives is given to us by God. When we fail to realize that God gives us the purpose for our lives, we will waste our time pursuing our own life goals and ambitions without ever experiencing a true sense of accomplishment or feeling fulfilled in our lives.

As we begin looking at the power of purpose, we are going to examine the book of Jonah.

## *Running from Your Purpose*

In the book of Jonah, God tells Jonah to go preach against the wickedness of Nineveh. Jonah doesn't want to do it, so he goes in the opposite direction to do something else. How many times has God told you to do something that you didn't want to do? How many times did you know you were supposed to be doing one thing but decided to do something else instead?

When God speaks to us and tells us to do something and we don't do it, we're doing exactly what Jonah did. We may not be physically running as he did but spiritually we're running away from God. We're running away because we're not fulfilling our purpose.

Jonah was a prophet. A prophet is the mouthpiece of God; meaning that when a prophet speaks, you should take what they are saying just as if it is coming from God Himself. Why? Because a true prophet of God does not speak their own will, they speak what God reveals to them to speak.

A prophet speaks from the heart of God. When God reveals something to the prophet to speak to His people, He's revealing what's in His heart to His people.

Since Jonah is a prophet of God and the mouthpiece of God, the fact that he ran in the opposite direction of Nineveh; refusing to go means that he was running away from fulfilling the very purpose he was created to fulfill...speaking to the people on behalf of God. Only you can fulfill your purpose, nobody else can do what God created you to do.

In 2013, the United States celebrated the 50th Anniversary of the March on Washington. We can look back over history and see that there were many powerful and influential leaders, celebrities and preachers doing remarkable things during the civil rights movement. However, Martin Luther King was created for being a national leader for the movement. Nobody else could have done what he did.

Nobody else could speak to Nineveh and be heard like Jonah. Had anybody else went with God's message, they probably would have been rejected; and Jonah knew this, which is why he didn't want to go.

Nineveh was part of the Assyrian empire, a group that had continuously invaded Israel, plundered resources from Israel, and harassed Israel. Jonah hated the Assyrians because of the aggression they brought towards him and his people. Jonah probably wanted to see the Assyrian's punished by God and may have felt if he did not give them God's message they eventually would be, so he ran. He buys a ticket, hops a ship and heads for Tarshish.

## ***Rejecting Our Purpose Leads to Turmoil***

Jonah hopped a boat trying to run from God; run from his purpose to Tarshish. God could not allow Jonah to make it to Tarshish. If Jonah had made it to Tarshish it would send a message to the world that you can reject God's purpose for your life and successfully pursue your own. (*See Jonah 1:4*)

When we reject God's assignment for our lives to pursue our own agenda, and our own objectives, we face obstacles because God is not going to allow us to prosper in our plans and endeavors when we reject His. When God gives us an assignment and we try to run from it, we run in to all types of obstacles that make it impossible for us to be successful in what we're trying to do. That's part of the *power behind purpose.*

The purpose for your life is too great to let you be successful in getting away from it. This is also why it's important to know God's purpose for your life; because you can be dealing with obstacles your whole life and not realize that it's because you're going against the grain of what God has created you to do.

You're wondering why nothing you put your hands to is prospering like the Word of God says its suppose to *(See Deut. 28:8)* but you must understand that everything you put your hands to shall prosper only when you're acting in accordance with God's will and purpose for your life.

## *Purpose & Fruit*

In the gospel of Matthew, Jesus was going into the city and when He got hungry and saw a fig tree, He went to get fruit from the tree to satisfy His hunger. However, the fig tree had no fruit causing Jesus to curse the fig tree declaring that from this point on no fruit will ever grow on this tree (*See Matthew 21:18*).

Many people have read this verse of scripture and wondered why Jesus cursed this fig tree. The reason Jesus cursed this tree was because the fruit of the fig tree normally began to appear at the same time as the leaves first appeared on the fig tree. Since the leaves of this fig tree had already appeared to be in full bloom, it indicated that there should also be fruit on this tree that was already growing.

However, upon arriving at the tree and seeing that no fruit has grown, Jesus curses the tree. Jesus' actions here have a symbolic importance which signify the hypocrisy of all who have the appearance that they are bearing fruit but in fact are not.

Like the fig tree, God created all of us with a purpose. But we must examine ourselves and what we are doing in life to make sure we are in fact bearing fruit related to the purpose that God created us for or if we simply have the *appearance* of bearing fruit. If we are not careful, we will live our lives caught up with trying to obtain *"The American Dream"* without placing any focus on the main purpose for which God created us. God created us to give Him glory by serving Him in various capacities.

However, if we don't know in what capacity God wants us to serve, we could be presenting an image of bearing fruit when, we are just a tree with fully blossomed leaves and no fruit.

It must be understood that when a fig tree produces fruit, the fruit is not there simply so the tree can look beautiful. The fruit is there so that those who partake of the fruit the tree has produces can eat from the tree; the tree produces sustenance that will help them maintain their life.

Our life is not solely about us, it's about fulfilling the purpose for which God placed us here because somebody somewhere needs the fruit that you should be producing to help them maintain their life just as our life is sustained by the fruit produced by others. God has also placed people in your life that should be producing good fruit that helps you to maintain your life. What they produce around you should build you up spiritually as well as encourage and motivate you to pursue your destiny in God.

However, we have allowed too many people for far too long to remain planted around us with fully bloomed leaves and no fruit. They provide no sustenance to us but are a consistent drain to us. We must begin to take the mentality that Jesus took with the fig tree.

We must examine the people around us and identify the fruit they are producing into our lives. If they are not producing the fruit that's a blessing to us, we must remove them from our inner circle so that God can replace them with someone who will.

However, we must also examine ourselves to ensure that we are not only draining the fruit from the lives of other but are also producing fruit that is a blessing to those around us as well.

# Chapter 3

## IDENTITY & PURPOSE

*"Before I formed you in the womb I knew you, before you were born I set you apart; I appointed you as a prophet to the nations."*
— Jeremiah 1:5

Before our lives began, God had a purpose for us. He had already consecrated or set us aside to fulfill that purpose before He ever established the foundations of the Earth or any of creation. What we must understand is that God didn't make man to be a part of creation. God made all of creation for man; for man's pleasure and enjoyment. Since God made all of creation for mankind, before the thought of creation entered the mind of God, the thought of mankind; the thought of each and everyone one of us was already occupying His mind.

As God thought of creating us, He then thought about creating the Heavens above, the Earth and the fullness thereof and the seas below. When God made all of creation, He had a purpose for each one of us to fulfill within it.

So, I pose this question: What is your purpose? Why are you here? What did God create you to do? There's a reason why you were born into the family you're in. There's a reason you have the level of education that you have. There's a reason behind why you've had and are having your life experiences. Whether good or bad, traumatic or pleasing, there is a reason.

The mistakes you've made in life play a role in helping to mold and shape you into the person you need to be so that you are equipped to walk your path of destiny and fulfill your purpose. We've always been taught by society; taught by the world that our life is our own and we must do what makes us happy. We've been taught to excel and achieve goals to gain our own personal fulfillment, self-worth, inner peace and joy within life. But billions of people have done that since the beginning of time and most were still unhappy.

Many successful business people will tell you that they put in countless hours, worked through vacations and holidays to climb the ladder of their respective industry only to get to the top and still feel that something was missing from their life. Many millionaires and other financially comfortable people will tell you that while they enjoy the lifestyle their money allows them to have, there are times when there still seems to be something missing from their life; something that money cannot buy.

It's not until we realize that our life is not about us but about serving God for others and we are willing to accept that truth to the point that we are willing to walk away from everything else that hinders us from serving God that we begin to understand what is important in life. Purpose!

It's not until we start fulfilling the purpose for which God created us that we truly become happy with life and feel no emptiness.

Our purpose is not about us, but about how God is going to use us for the benefit of others. How do we know this? We know this because it says so in the scripture above (*See Jeremiah 1:5*). The text says before I formed you in the womb I knew you. This means before creation, God had you and your life on His mind.

It goes on to say that I consecrated and appointed you a prophet to the nations. Here God is telling Jeremiah the purpose for which He created him. He consecrated him and appointed him to be a prophet to the nations. Consecration means to be set apart. God has set each of us apart for His work.

Now, some of you might know you're supposed to be serving God but are not sure in what capacity. Others may not realize that God has a divine purpose for your life. You might have everything together in your life. And with everything going exactly the way you want it to in your life, at times you might still feel an emptiness; a void or as if something is still missing from your life. In either case, you will not find satisfaction in your life until you know the purpose for your life.

## *Finding Your Purpose*

As we look at how we find our purpose, we may begin to understand some of the events that have transpired in our lives and why we've had to go through some of the things we've gone through. To do this, let's look at the life of Moses.

During the time of Moses, the Hebrews in Egypt began to outnumber the Egyptians. The new Egyptian Pharaoh believed the growing population of Hebrews to be a threat to their national security. He believed if a time of war came, the Hebrews could rebel and join with Egypt's enemies and overtake Egypt.

So, the first thing Pharaoh did was enslaved all the Hebrews. Then Pharaoh went to the Hebrew midwives; the women who helped pregnant Hebrew women deliver their babies, and instructed them that when they assisted in a delivery to pay attention to the sex of the baby born. If it was a son, they were to kill it but if it was a daughter, she could live. Pharaoh gave this decree because the more Hebrew men born meant a greater threat to Egypt because men fought wars.

Now what looked on the surface to be a fearful king taking steps to ensure national security was Satan behind the scenes attempting to manipulate spiritual events.

We all know that the Hebrews were God's chosen nation. Satan would do anything to destroy what God favors. So, Satan began speaking to the mind of Pharaoh with persuasive arguments, opinions and suggestions until he manipulated him into enslaving an entire nation of people. It's not a coincidence that this now enslaved nation of people was God's chosen people.

Satan understands that God works through mankind to accomplish His purposes in the Earth, so the first thing Satan did was manipulate Pharaoh into trying to kill all the newborn boys. Why? Because Satan believes for God to set His people free, He's going to have to raise up a generation of men to fight for their release. Satan's belief is that enslaved men are not going to rebel, if they were, they would have done so to prevent themselves from becoming slaves in the first place since the Hebrews already greatly outnumbered the Egyptians.

Satan believed that he didn't have to worry about them. What he did have to worry about was a new man being born and becoming a deliverer to the Hebrews inspiring them to rebel, so he decides to have all the new baby boys killed.

## *Your Purpose*

The first thing you must know about finding your purpose is that the enemy wants to destroy you before you can ever get to a point in your life to even discover you have a purpose. This is why traumatic experiences and events happen in your life. This is why you've had to endure certain hardships at times in your life. The enemy is trying to destroy you to prevent God from bringing you to a place of knowing the purpose of your life.

Many of these events are completely beyond our control. There's nothing we've done or didn't do to bring these events upon us, it's simply that Satan sought you out and through others tried to destroy your life to prevent you from living your life; the life God desires you to have. The enemy doesn't want you to ever discover your purpose.

The day that you discover your God given purpose for being on this Earth and being marching towards your destiny in fulfilling that purpose is the day you start taking territory for God's Kingdom right out of the hands of the enemy.

Because you have a purpose; a destiny, the enemy begins to fight against you to overtake you; trying to destroy you before you ever know what that purpose is. Satan may not know the purpose *on* your life, but he does know there is a purpose *for* your life and if he can destroy you with life threatening or life shattering events, he can destroy you from ever walking your path of destiny to fulfill the purpose for your life; the purpose for which God created you.

## ***Birthing Purpose***

When we look back at the birth of Moses, we see that the midwives feared God, so they didn't kill any of the children that were born (*See Exodus 1:17*). Because of this, Moses the future deliverer of Egypt could be born. Since the midwives did not kill the newborn boys, Pharaoh ordered every Hebrew son to be thrown into the Nile River (*See Exodus 1:22*).

As Pharaoh attempted to have every male child thrown in the Nile River, Moses' mother hid him for 3 months to prevent his death. When she could no longer hide him, she put him in a basket and floated him down the river. Pharaoh's sister found the basket and raised Moses as her own son (*See Exodus 2:1-10*).

What the enemy means for our bad, God means for our God. God doesn't desire that any should suffer, but most of us cannot deny the fact that had we not faced trying times filled with suffering in our lives, we wouldn't know God like we do. We never would have sought God out or called on Him for comfort. While the enemy was trying to break you and destroy you, God was molding you and shaping you into a vessel that was fit for His service and capable of fulfilling a purpose.

Therefore, we cannot give up in life because things get too hard. We cannot give up when the enemy begins to challenge us with devastating events. The enemy wants to destroy you before you ever get to a place to know or understand that God has a purpose for your life.

Therefore, it is important for us to introduce our children to God so that they know and understand the ways of God. Therefore, it is important for us to stay before God personally in prayer, meditation and personal study. Too many people have aborted the process of being prepared for their purpose because in their eyes, life got too hard to endure.

They stopped pushing forward and striving because they didn't realize that in the midst of their storms, in the midst of their struggles, God has His hands all over them molding and shaping them into a stronger vessel. So rather than live a life of purpose, they live a life of self-fulfillment; bitter of past experiences and never know true fulfillment or purpose.

So, the first thing we need to learn when it comes to finding our purpose is that we cannot abort the process of God molding and shaping us to be a vessel fit for His use, no matter how difficult life gets, we must keep pushing forward to get be in His presence.

# Chapter 4

## IDENTITY INFLUENCES BEHAVIOR

*"But you are a chosen people, a royal priesthood, a holy nation, God's special possession, that you may declare the praises of Him who called you out of darkness into His wonderful light"*

- 1 Peter 2:9

Who are you? If you were asked that question, what would your answer be? Would you begin by stating your name? Giving your name would not be an adequate answer because the question is who are you, not what is your name?

Would you answer the question by stating your profession, your race, your skills or abilities? I'm a doctor, I'm a plumber, I'm retired; I'm black, I'm white, I'm Hispanic, I like to cook, I like to draw. These too would be inadequate answers as they give descriptions of what you do and what you look like but still does not answer the question of who you are?

To answer the question of who you are, you must know your identity. Your identity can only be found in Jesus Christ. Even with that understanding, you still may not be able to answer the question of who are you. See, many will take the fact that you can only know your identity through Jesus Christ and answer the question by simply stating; I am a child of God.

Although that sounds like a great answer to the question, it would be an incorrect answer. See, we are all children of God; we are all sinners who have been saved by grace. But just like your fingerprint is unique to you, your identity in Christ is unique to you as well. Your identity in Christ is unique to you and can only be known through your personal relationship with Him.

When you are asked the question who are you, your answer should be just as unique as your fingerprint because your identity is known through revelation by fellowship with the one who first established and gave you your identity. Your relationship with Jesus should be unique to you making your identity in Him unique to you.

## *When Identity Becomes Idolatry*

When we don't know our *identity*, we begin to operate in *idolatry*. Idolatry is the worship of idols or excessive devotion to or reverence for someone or something. An idol is anything that replaces the one true God as first in our lives. God created us to give Him glory. God created us to praise and worship Him.

To give God glory, to praise and worship God in spirit and in truth, He must come first in our lives. He must come before *everything*. God must come before our jobs, our hobbies, our desires, our spouses, our children, our finances. Everything that our flesh; or our natural mind leads us to believe is important must take a backseat to God; everything in our lives must take a backseat to God. Anything that we place more value, more importance or give more priority to over God becomes an idol and we get caught up in the practice of idolatry rather than the discovery of our identity.

During biblical times, people would mostly practice idolatry by worshipping false man-made gods. They would worship gods made of gold, or gods made to look half human and half animal, and they presented sacrifices to these false gods and prayed to them. However, today the enemy and the sin within us is a lot subtler. We're too smart and God has revealed too much of Himself today for us to be foolish enough to worship and sacrifice to golden calves, and images of birds and wooden dolls that we've made with our own hands.

But idolatry continues to be one of the most sinful practices in the lives of mankind today, including the life of Christians. Each day, if we are not careful and in most cases, we are not; we practice idolatry; placing God on the back burner while granting excessive devotion and reverence to other things in our lives. Surprisingly, the number one idol we have in our lives today is not our money, it's not our job, it's not some false god that we purposefully pray to or worship. The number one idol we have in our lives today is *ourselves.*

## *I'm My Own Idol*

When we don't know our identity, we begin to operate in idolatry. We begin to seek out our identity from within ourselves to define who we are without God. To define who we are without God, we build our own identity in our own eyes of who we perceive we are.

As a Christian, whenever you hear someone talking negatively about God, it sparks a certain anger in you. It sparks that anger in you because they are tearing down that which you hold dear. When you hear somebody saying God cannot be real because science clearly shows how the universe and everything within it was created it may lead you to say, "they're stupid," they don't know what they are talking about or many other things to that affect.

We respond in such a manner because we feel we must defend our God whom we hold dear because that is where we find our identity; that's where we find who we are. When God comes under attack our identity comes under attack and if God is not real; does not exist, then who are we and where do we get our identity? I am who I am because of God so when you attack God, you attack who I am.

Just as we would defend God when He comes under attack, when we don't know our identity, we defend ourselves when we come under attack because sin drives us to seek our identity from within ourselves rather than through coming to God. Therefore, the bible is so adamant about denying yourself. When you deny yourself to embrace God you block sin from driving you to make yourself your own idol. Jesus said turn the other cheek (*See Matthew 5:39*).

You turn the other cheek because when you seek to avenge wrong done unto you, you set yourself up to make yourself your own idol. Jesus tells us to love those who spitefully use you (*See Luke 6:28*). Again, when you hate those who take advantage of you, you operate in sin from a place of idolatry.

## *How I Become My Idol*

How is it that we make ourselves our own idol? Let's look at it from a relationship perspective. As adults, many of us have endured a heartbreak or two in our lives; possibly more. We've been dumped, cheated on, taken advantage of in the various relationships of our lives; both men and women. But what do we do when our relationships end on a sour note? We don't say well, that just how it goes. No! We say things like; *"He cheated on me with her!"* or *"She won't find nobody as good as me!"* *"He won't find anybody that's going treat him like I did!"*

As we vent our frustrations about the way the relationship ended, we tend to think of this as coping with the breakup. However, what's taking place is that our ego; which is our inward feeling of self-importance has been damaged during the breakup. To heal our ego and restore our self-importance in our own eyes, we try to convince ourselves that something must be wrong with the person we broke up with because that's the only way to justify them not wanting to be with someone as amazing as us, so we must massage, caress, heal and repair our ego because we find our identity or self-importance in it. When we know who we are in Christ and our identity; or how we view ourselves our worth is not diminished during a breakup.

Let's look at this in a different way. Let's say someone enters a room and they don't speak to you. What you are the thoughts going through your head? Maybe something like; *"I don't know what they problem is? They're just rude. The least they could do was speak to me."* We don't take into consideration the things that could possibly be going on in this person life that could have led to them not speaking. They could be deep in thought and didn't even notice you; they could be having an unpleasant day and feel rejected by the world and really need somebody to speak life into them. But all we are concerned with is the fact that we are in the room and they entered in without speaking to us.

We call it our ego but, it is our idol; the idol of ourselves that has been insulted. The value of our identity has been insulted because this person didn't speak to us. We've given ourselves an identity of importance in our own eyes and when someone does not live up to or approach us with the level of value and importance that we place on our own selves, our identity is placed into question.

When we become our own idol, rather than God being first in our lives, we place ourselves first and internally believe that everything revolves around us and must meet our standard of appropriateness. When things don't meet our standard of appropriateness, we, or our idol is insulted because it was not given the proper worship we believe should have been given. To validate the identity, we've given ourselves, rather than realize that the problem is with us because we're idolizing ourselves; we place the blame at the feet of others.

Our identity can only be found in Jesus. To search for identity anywhere else leads to idolatry, and when the value of where we draw our idolatrous identity comes under attack, it leads us to defend it because it is an attack on the self-centeredness of who we think we are.

# DARRIUS GETER

# Chapter 5

## NEGATIVE IDENTITY

*"And Moses said unto God, 'Who am I, that I should go unto Pharaoh, and that I should bring forth the children of Israel out of Egypt?'"*

- Exodus 3:11

Our identity; our perception of who we are influences our lives. Whatever we think about ourselves becomes our reality, so our very own perceived self-identity produces either a negative or positive outcome for our lives; a successful life or a life filled with turmoil is greatly determined by our own perceived self-identity.

How many times have you defeated yourself before you even started because you convinced yourself you didn't deserve to be happy, you didn't deserve to be promoted, or you disqualified yourself because you didn't think you were smart enough, strong enough or didn't have enough confidence in yourself or your own abilities? How many times have we placed ourselves at a disadvantage; not because we were at a disadvantage but simply because we perceived we were based on our own flawed self-identity?

## *The Burning Bush*

When Moses met God at the burning bush and was instructed to go tell Pharaoh to let God's people go, Moses disqualified himself from the assignment due to his own flawed self-identity which was based on his own perception of himself and not on who he was through God (*See Exodus 3*). When we know who we are through God, we realize that no assignment, vision, mission or dream is impossible to us because our success is not based on our own abilities or who we are on our own but in God who empowers us to be successful and victorious.

So often, we allow others and society to dictate and determine the standards of what acceptable self-identity looks like, of what being capable looks like. When we accept societal standards and the conceived standards of others as the bar that must be reached or achieved to measure up to an acceptable status, what we are doing is allowing others to determine our identity and who we should be. God created each of us to be unique individuals, so why should we subscribe to a worldly uniformity of what's considered to be an acceptable identity?

## ***Burning Bush Revelation***

As Moses continued to disqualify himself to God by stating how unequipped he was to be used as the deliverer of Israel, God began to reveal to Moses his identity in God. There are two things God revealed to Moses that helped Moses discover his identity in God. The first thing God told Moses to help him discover his identity was that He would be with Moses (*See Exodus 3:12*).

When we judge ourselves according to the standards of the world and try to define our identity from within, it's difficult for us to believe that we can accomplish remarkable things because we feel alone. When we attempt to accomplish great tasks, we feel more comfortable with others working with us. The presence of others provides us a certain level of comfort.

However, the purpose for our lives is our own. God created us for a purpose unique to us and because of that, we must be willing to begin the journey alone. The fact that God is with us no matter what gives us the confidence we need to start any journey, assignment, mission or dream because we are not alone; He is with us.

The second thing that God told Moses to help him discover his identity was that He is I AM (*See Exodus 3:14*). Many times, we lack confidence in our ability to do something because we believe we have no voice or authority that can rally others to follow us, get them to listen to us or respect us. As God is telling Moses to go tell Pharaoh to let the Hebrews go, Moses is thinking who am I to go to the most powerful king in the Earth right now and demand that he let his slaves go free.

When we recognize that God *IS*...we draw confidence in our identity through Him and begin to know and understand that nothing is too hard, difficult or impossible for us. We grow confident because we recognize that we are walking in God's authority which is higher than any authority. We recognize that whatever we need to be successful or victorious, we can receive it because God is with us and God *IS* the very thing that we need. God *IS* the very thing that we lack when our natural mind or worldly standards tell disqualifies us or makes us feel unequipped. Our identity in God is bolstered by the revelation that wherever we are weak, unequipped or lacking is made up by God who *makes* us strong, equipped or sufficient because He *IS* the great *I AM*.

# Chapter 6

## BROKENNESS

*"My spirit is broken, my days are cut short, the grave awaits me."*

- Job 17:1

We are all broken in some area or areas of our lives. One of the main reasons we draw closer to God is to get a fuller revelation of who we are; to obtain our full identity so that we can become a whole person in God rather than remain a broken person without Him. Although we are all broken in some area or areas of our lives, we are not all broken in the same manner.

Because God created us as unique individuals, similar experiences produce within us unique perspectives. If you dropped two similar drinking glasses on the floor, they would be broken in two diverse ways.

The experiences in my life that make me broken may be the same experiences as yours but it may not affect your life in the same manner as it affects mine. To be broken means a person reaches a point in their life where they believe they are beyond repair. Brokenness can also bring into your life with it a plethora of additional mental states such as low self-esteem, lack of confidence, lack of self-respect, depression and many others. Brokenness plays such a key role in how we view ourselves and develop a negative perception of our self-identity.

The experiences we've accumulated over a lifetime; going back as far as our childhood help to shape our self-identity when we become adults.

However, everything we experienced in our childhood was not for our benefit and in many cases, have produced scars on our spirit that have and continue to negatively influence the course of our lives by redefining our identity from what God desires it to be.

Scars from rejection, broken trust, mistreatment, being molested or raped and many others have penetrated our lives and manifested in various areas of our lives and influence the course of our lives by shaping who we are, what we believe and how we view ourselves and the world around us.

Because the various areas of brokenness in our lives shape how we see ourselves, our abilities and our limitations, the brokenness in our lives hinders the course of our lives because of the personal beliefs it produces in our heart about ourselves. Scars from our past influence the development of a negative self-identity because of the way it leads us to view life as well as ourselves.

## *We Are What We Think*

The experiences in our life influence the way we think about ourselves and the world around us. Because life experiences can shape the way we think, it is important that we view our experiences through the lenses of the Word of God and not through the lenses of the world or our natural way of thinking and understanding. The bible tells us in Proverbs 23:7, "*As a man thinks in his heart, so is he...*" This verse of scripture is straight-forward.

A person's life reflects how they think. The way I think about my life is what will manifest in my life. Therefore, the bible tells us to renew our minds daily, so that we think in line with the Word of God rather than any manner contrary to it. We get to know God personally through His Word, and we find our identity in Him through His Word. If we think contrary to God Word, we are thinking contrary to our very identity.

So, looking at that verse of scripture from Proverbs 23:7 and a few other passages throughout the bible, we can see the importance of thinking of ourselves as God sees us and not how we feel about us. Again, Proverbs 23:7 tells us that "as a man thinks in his heart, so is he..." This verse of scripture tells us 3 things:

> First: It tells us that we originate our thoughts in our minds.
>
> Second: Whatever we begin to think, we believe and we take it to heart.
>
> Third: Whatever we think in our heart is what we become.

The Bible also tells us that the mouth speaks from the abundance of the heart (*See Luke 6:45*). That means that the things we say about our life are what we believe about our life. The things we say about our situation are what we believe about our situation. The things we say about our plans and our goals are what we believe about our plans and our goals.

The Bible also again tells us that the power of death and life are in the tongue (*See Proverbs 18:21*). This means that we give life to whatever we say including giving life to negativity, failure, destruction, disappointment and even death. The Bible also tells us in Proverbs 4:23 that the issues of life flow from what's in our heart. This means the nature of our life conditions reflect what's in our heart.

- *Since we give death or life to whatever we speak*
- *And whatever we speak comes from what's in our heart*
- *And the issues of life spring out from what's in our heart*
- *And what's in our heart is determined by the thoughts that originate in our minds...*

We need to make sure we renew our minds daily to focus on God and the finished works of Jesus. See, our thoughts determine our actions and our life reflects our actions. For instance, if I wanted to start a business and I focused on my shortcomings and all the negative things I believe about myself rather than how I am empowered through Jesus then I'm going to spend most of my time believing that my business is going to fail due to my negative self-identity.

I may want my business to succeed but if I don't believe in my heart that it's going to be successful due to my perceived shortcomings, it will fail. Why would it fail? Because in my heart, I never believed it would be successful due to my own perceived shortcomings or my own flawed self-identity that made me think I was not capable.

Since I did not believe it would be successful, I would not put forth the necessary actions to position my business for success because in my own mind, I would have already told myself that I'm not capable of adequately doing everything necessary to be successful. As a man thinks in his heart, so is he... *(See*

*Proverbs 23:7*). As I thought in my heart, so was I in my business pursuit...A failure.

## *Change Your Consciousness*

Our life reflects our consciousness; how we see ourselves. Do we see ourselves as God sees us or through our own flawed eyes which has been shaped by the brokenness we have experienced throughout our life? Here's a simple statement; *"Change Your Consciousness and you will Change Your Life."*

If you can change what you think and believe about yourself; removing your flawed self-identity and begin to see yourself as God sees you, you will begin to see your life line up with exactly what you believe about yourself because it will be exactly what God desires for you because it's how God sees you.

# Chapter 7

## CREATING OUR OWN IDENTITY

*"When the woman saw that the fruit of the tree was good for food and pleasing to the eye, and also desirable for gaining wisdom, she took some and ate it. She also gave some to her husband, who was with her, and he ate it. Then the eyes of both of them were opened, and they realized they were naked; so they sewed fig leaves together and made coverings for themselves."*

– Genesis 3:6-7

In the above scripture, God placed in the Garden of Eden every tree and green plant that would be appealing to the eye for *beauty* and for *food*. Still, Adam and Eve decided to disobey God's direct command to refrain from partaking of the Tree of The Knowledge of Good and Evil and they helped themselves to that which has been classified as forbidden.

Immediately after sharing in an afternoon snack from this forbidden tree, the bible says that Adam and Eve *knew* that they were *naked*. Although Adam and Eve were *physically* naked in the Garden of Eden, the nakedness that they felt was not a *physical* nakedness but it was a *spiritual* nakedness.

To understand how they felt a spiritual nakedness in the Garden of Eden, we must first understand the nature of the tree they chose to eat from. You see this tree was no ordinary fruit tree. The tree was called the Tree of The Knowledge of Good and Evil. If you pulled an apple from and apple tree you got an Apple. If you pulled an orange from and orange tree you got an orange. But whosoever partook of the fruit from *this* tree would get knowledge of what was *good* and what was *evil*.

From the moment that Adam and Eve ate the fruit from this forbidden tree, they *knew* that what they had done was evil. Upon the realization that they had just broken God's command, they felt *naked* in the spiritual because the *covering* of God was no longer upon them. Not only did they lose their innocent, they also lost their identity.

The loss of their spiritual covering from God meant that they were cut off from their *provider*, their *protector*, their *peace giver*, their *joy*, their *happiness*, the *lover of their soul*, the *giver of their life*, the one from whom they received their *identity*. Because of this great loss, they also felt *ashamed*. So, they used the *physical* item of a fig leaf to cover their physical bodies to hide their *spiritual shame*. What they didn't realize was that only the Lord could hide their shame.

## *Shame and False Identity*

As time has progressed from the Fall of Man in the Garden of Eden on up to the redemption of man with the crucifixion Christ all the way up to now, mankind continues to use physical items to hide spiritual shame. Shame is a painful feeling caused by the consciousness of being exposed as unworthy because of our conduct or our circumstances. Although we have been redeemed by Jesus and in Him there is no shame, we still experience spiritual shame when we are disconnected from God.

When we are disconnected from God we feel shame because we lack the knowledge of our proper identity. When we lack proper identity, we can live a boring, uneventful life; always desiring to do more and be more without ever achieving it because we've devalued our ability to accomplish it due to a lack of proper identity.

When we talk about spiritual shame, we are talking about areas in our life where we are lacking the presence of God. When we do not see ourselves as God sees us certain areas in our lives are painful for us to look at because we feel exposed and naked to the world because we are not measuring up to the standard that we know we should be.

In an unconscious attempt to hide from the world the fact that we don't know our identity in those areas, we find something in the physical to make us appear to the world as if we know who we are. We create a false identity to hide the fact that we are lost and don't know who we are in God.

## *Covering Our Shame*

When it comes to covering our shame by creating a false identity, there are multiple ways in which we try to do it. However, I believe that there are three ways that are most common. The three most common ways we create a false identity to hide from the world that we don't really know who we are, is *financially*, *relationally*, and *testimony*.

## ***Creating a False Financial Identity***

The first way we attempt to create a false identity is financially. In today's economy, it takes money to live. You need money to eat, money to have a roof over your head, money to put clothes on your back. It even takes money to go to work and make money. However, when we don't know our identity in God, God is not represented in our finances which lead us to have no financial peace. Since we have no financial peace, we begin to feel financially ashamed.

When we become financially ashamed, we may start to think that if I'm not driving the best car, living in the biggest house in the most upscale neighborhood and wearing top designer clothes, I'll be viewed as a lacking financially, so we buy these things so we will not feel ashamed because we are seeking to find identity through finances.

What we fail to realize is that our spirit is crying out to us because we do not know our identity in Christ. Just as Eve saw that the fruit from the Tree of Knowledge was pleasant to the eye, we look for physical items that are pleasant to our eyes and good for making us look financially prosperous. So, we buy cars we cannot pay the note on and take out mortgages we cannot afford which leads to foreclosure. And if it's not a name brand suit or designer dress we don't want anything to do with it. We ruin our credit trying to keep up with the Jones' to hide our financial shame.

When we put God in our finances, He gives us wisdom to understand that true wealth is not determined by how much you have, but how little you need. And whatever need you have, God is faithful and just to provide it. When we know God as *JEHOVAH – JIREH;* God our Provider (*See Genesis 22:14*) and that our identity in *Him* is what makes us prosperous and not the material things we have, we will no longer be financially ashamed.

## ***Creating a False Relational Identity***

The second way we attempt to hide our spiritual shame is *relationally*, especially in love. Galatians 5:22 identifies love as being a fruit of the Spirit; meaning that if you don't know your identity in God then you do not know what love is. God created us to be relational beings, but when we don't know our identity our soul cries out in shame.

To hide this shame in our lives, many of us have surrounded ourselves with four or five girlfriends or boyfriends to keep us *company*; satisfying our physical needs because on the inside we lack our identity in God which tells us how valuable we are. The void of knowing who we are in God makes us lonely. When the novelty of the current lover we have chosen to keep around us has worn off, we put them to the side and find a replacement that will excite us all over again.

Because we lack the fruit of love from the Spirit, we don't care anything about the feelings of the ones we just put aside, or how much we hurt them, nor do we care about the ones we are bringing into our loveless lives because we are seeking to hide our shame by temporarily filling a void in our lives that only the love of God can fill.

What we need to do instead of jumping from bed to bed is get to know the one Ezekiel called JEHOVAH – SHAMAH; The Lord is There, (*See Ezekiel 48:35*). It's not until we allow the Spirit of God to put love in our hearts that we will know our identity in God and be able to fill the void of love in our lives by feeling the love of God in our lives.

## *False Identity Through Testimony*

Now that we've talked about *financial shame* and *relational shame*, the third area I want to talk to you about where we attempt to hide the shame of not knowing our identity; which is in our *testimony*. Our testimony is our opportunity to tell other Christians and even non-believers about the power of God and how we have seen it work from experience in our own lives.

The Christian testimony is a powerful thing because it inspires other believers and even some non-believers to seek to know God in the manner we have testified that we have seen him operate within. However, it has been most of our experience that we have come to know God and see him operate miraculously in our lives while we were enduring some of the ugliest times of our lives.

Rather than provide testimony on these situations of our lives, we physically forbid testimony by refusing to open our mouths and speak because we are embarrassed to show anyone just how much of the spirit of God we are lacking in certain areas of our life because we don't want anybody to see our shame.

We hide our testimony because we don't want anyone to know that we don't have everything together in our lives. We don't want people to know that there are still area's in our lives where we don't know who we are; don't know our identity. What we fail to realize is that the work that God has done in our lives are a magnificent work and is something to be shouted about; because not only did God bring us through those ugly situations, but if we would just open your mouths and testify, God can remove the shame we feel internally of not knowing our identity.

Many of us believe that by sharing our experiences with others, especially someone we don't know, that they may begin to look at us differently because we've shown them a glimpse of our shame; our false identity. We've gone through great expense trying to look financially prosperous even though we were broke, and we've given the appearance that our lives are filled with great love even though we cannot hold a meaningful conversation with any of our *"friends with benefits"* let alone have a positive meaningful relationship with anyone else because inside we don't even know who we are.

We have tried to portray the image that we don't have any problems, any struggles or any issues in our lives and if we tell somebody just how ugly our situation really is, they'll think we are nothing but a phony Christian.

When we endure struggles and our hardships they help us to learn who we are in God because they bring us closer to God, they make us stronger, we learned to trust God in that area of our life; meaning we learn who we are, we learn our identity in God and we gain purpose in our lives be we now hold the blue print to help somebody else get through the same situations we've faced helping them discover their identity in God as well.

# DARRIUS GETER

# Chapter 8

## QUESTIONING YOUR WORTH

*"Finally, brethren, whatever things are true, whatever things are noble, whatever things are just, whatever things are pure, whatever things are lovely, whatever things are of good report, if there is any virtue and if there is anything praiseworthy- meditate on these things."*

- Philippians 4:8

There was a woman who found herself in an abusive relationship. She didn't know how she got there, it was as if one day she woke up and realized she was living her life in a prison and didn't know how to get out. Her boyfriend would beat her relentlessly for even the smallest of what he called "infractions," and in many cases verbally abused her while he physically abused her.

This woman grew up in a loving home and was never physically abused by her parents. Her personality was pleasant, and her friends would say that "she wouldn't hurt a fly." Because she was the sweetest person, her friends couldn't understand why her boyfriend was so cruel to her nor did they understand why she allowed herself to be subjugated to such a horrific relationship. Her friends and family pleaded with her to get out of this relationship, but she would not. When they asked her why she continued to stay with a man who was so harsh to her, her only response was simply, "Without him, I'd be alone."

Rather than be alone, this woman preferred to remain in an abusive relationship. She could not see within herself what so many other people around her saw...her worth.

Knowing who you are affords you the knowledge of knowing your worth. When you don't know who you are, you are more likely to sell yourself for less that you are worth. When you don't know the value of who you are, you will allow yourself to be mistreated, degraded, and walked over because you don't believe you are entitled to better. We all deserve the best out of life and to be treated the best by the people around us, but if we don't know our identity in Christ, we will not demand to be treated or respected with the full value of what we are worth.

Self-worth is defined as "the sense of one's own value or worth as a person." A person's value or worth is determined by how they view their self; in other words, you determine what you are worth. So how do you begin the process of appraising your self-worth?

## **Appraising Your Self Worth**

Anyone who has ever purchased a home know that one of the first things you do is have the prospective property appraised. When an appraiser examines a home, they inspect the foundation and all other outside structures. They also inspect the homes interior and its amenities. The appraiser focuses his attention on specific areas of the home ensuring that due diligence is conducted on your prospective home so that you know its true value.

In Philippians, the Apostle Paul gives us a checklist of areas on which to focus our attention as we appraise our own self-worth and value. For others to know our value, we first must know the value within ourselves. However, when it comes to assessing our self-value, many of us tend to focus on the negative aspects of who we are rather than the positive. When we focus on the negative, we begin to lower the value of who we are because we believe we inherently deserve to devalue ourselves because of the undesirable aspects of our life. This is the reason the Apostle Paul instructs us to focus on the positive things.

## *Whatever Things Are True*

When we focus on the positive things about ourselves, we feel good about ourselves and we increase our self-value and self-worth. Focusing on the good things about yourself does not mean you need to ignore the true negative things about yourself.

Paul tells us, "whatever things are true…" meditate on these things. When there is something true but negative about us, we should focus our attention on those things so that we can improve ourselves. We should not focus on negative things just to feel bad about who we are, but we should strive to improve and make the necessary changes in our life so that we can improve our self-value.

The Apostle Paul encourages us to meditate or ponder the good qualities of our life and our character. When we focus on the good qualities, we feel good about ourselves and are less likely to allow ourselves to be mistreated by others. But the question arises, how can we focus on the good things about our lives over the negative and not begin to puff ourselves up? Focusing on the positive qualities of who we are requires us to find our identity in Christ rather than the world's standard of positive qualities.

When we seek our identity in Christ for the Holy Spirit to direct our attention on the positive qualities of who we are, we remain humbled because we recognize it's Him who imparts the positive within us because the value of our self-worth comes from our identity in Jesus.

# IDENTITY

Many of the negative feelings we experience in life about ourselves can be attributed to the way we think about ourselves. So often, we focus on our shortcomings, our faults and our failures. We pay more attention to these negative aspects and they produce within us feelings of inadequacy. When a home appraiser discovers that a portion of your home is inadequate, it lowers the value of your home until it can be repaired.

Likewise, when we focus on the inadequacies within ourselves, we lower our self-worth, so we must renew our thinking about ourselves to ensure we maintain our personal value.

# Chapter 9

## YOU MUST DIE

*"Very truly I tell you, unless a kernel of wheat falls to the ground and dies, it remains only a single seed. But if it dies, it produces many seeds. Anyone who loves their life will lose it, while anyone who hates their life in this world will keep it for eternal life. Whoever serves me must follow me; and where I am, my servant also will be. My Father will honor the one who serves me."*
– John 12:24-26

We all want the power of God to flow freely through our lives. We want our prayers answered and I believer more than anything, we want the promises of God to manifest in our lives so that we are victorious over every situation we face. If we are honest with ourselves, some of the problems we face make us wish we were dead sometimes if only for a split second so that we wouldn't have to face the pressures that are associated with them.

During all this personal turmoil where we're waiting for God to do something to help us, quite honestly, God is waiting for us *to die*. God is saying, I know you want my power to flow freely through you, I know you want your prayers answered, and I know you want my promises to manifest and solve all your problems but none of that can happen. God is saying, until you die, I cannot do anything.

To understand the significance of what Jesus is saying in the above scripture, we must fully understand the concept of death. Death mean a separation. There are two deaths the bible talks about;

there is a *spiritual death* (*See Isaiah 59:2*) and there is a *physical death* (*See Ecclesiastes 12:7*).

In the book of Genesis, when God tells Adam and Eve if they eat fruit from the forbidden tree they would surely die (*See Genesis 2*), He was talking about a spiritual death; which is when the spirit of man is separated from the presence of God; which is why we needed a savior in Jesus to restore us to a right standing or re-establish our connection with God. However, the form of death in which we are more familiar is physical death; when the spirit separates from the body.

So, what does it mean when God says you must die? It means that you must die to yourself. There must be a separation from who you *think* you are from who you *really* are. So, ponder the question in your mind...*Who am I?*

What answers came to mind as your pondered that question? Many people immediately think of their job title, or they identify their self with a relationship such as a husband, wife, father or mother. Maybe you identified yourself by your personality or your favorite hobby.

These identity labels are useful, even necessary at times. They shape the way we act and feel (and the way people act and feel toward us) in just about every situation. But many of these labels are misleading, and none of them describe who you really are. The way you describe yourself is often with labels that are temporal. To understand who you really are, you must understand that what you are is eternal and no matter how much time passes and no matter what situations you face, you will always be that. It's an eternal characteristic trait that cannot be taken away from you.

# IDENTITY

Now, let me tell you who you *really* are. You're *dumb*. And until you die and separate yourself from all the things you think you are and accept what you really are, which is *dumb*, God cannot reveal to you who you really are. See, throughout the Bible, God refers to His followers as *sheep* and Jesus as the *shepherd*. Why? Because sheep are dumb animals. Sheep don't know where they are going or how to get there which is why they follow the shepherd. If sheep could talk and you were to ask them why they are traveling this route, they would say I'm just following the shepherd.

Sheep don't know what they are going to eat but they trust that the shepherd will feed them. Sheep don't know what they are going to drink but they trust that the shepherd, but they trust that the shepherd will lead them to water. Even though sheep are unintelligent, when they choose to follow the shepherd, they become quite intelligent.

The actual unintelligent sheep is the one not following the shepherd. They don't know where they are going, they don't know how to get there, and they are not sure if the direction they are taking is the right way to travel; but there they are walking *without* direction. God wants us to understand until we *die* from our way of thinking, our way of doing things, our way of believing we have all the answers and realize that left to ourselves we are unintelligent, He cannot help us.

There are eight things God wants to show us from the introductory scripture (*John 12:24-26*) about *dying to ourselves* so that we begin learning our identity in Him.

### 1. *Submission*
The first thing God is trying to show us is Submission.

*Very truly I tell you, unless a kernel of wheat falls to the ground and dies, it remains only a single seed. But if it dies, it produces many seeds. - John 12:24*

Right here Jesus tells us what we need to do to die to ourselves. The wheat represents us, and the ground is Jesus. The fact that He says the wheat must fall to the ground means that beforehand the wheat is above the ground, after falling to the ground into means the wheat is now under the ground.

Jesus is saying that you must place yourself under Him which means you must *submit* your life to Him. Submission means to place yourself under the authority of someone else. Whatever your personal life goals, agenda and way of doing things are, you must resign yourself from them and submit yourself to the mission and authority of Jesus Christ.

### 2. *Alone*
*Until you Die you remain Alone.*

The person who has not and does not submit to the authority of Jesus is alone which means that they are separated from the only source that can reveal their identity which will provide purpose.

*"it remains only a single seed" - John 12:24*

If you continue to do things your way without submitting to the authority of Jesus in your life you will remain alone. Being alone in this context means you're separated from the one who gives you identity. You will continue to pray and receive no answer, you will continue to ask for direction and get none and you will continue to walk by yourself through life. Why? If you're not going to live life according to your God ordained purpose, He cannot help you because God is not going to submit to your authority or your way of doing things.

This is where we are in many areas of our life, we want God to submit to us and He won't, and we keep asking Him why we keep dealing with the same mess repeatedly in our lives. The reason many of us don't submit to God is because we're used to being in control. We believe if we are not in control of every area of our life then our life won't work; but we don't realize that the life plans we've been operating according to is the plan we've solely design for ourselves and it's not working anyway.

When we submit to God we may not know exactly where we are going, how we are going to get there but by faith, we follow the shepherd and experience a life of excitement we never would have imagined.

### 3. Empowered to Prosper
### Brings forth much fruit
*Jesus said the wheat or the person that does die will bring forth much fruit.*

The person that submits to Jesus and follows His way of doing things becomes connected to the only source that empowers them to prosper and because of that, their actions are guided by the Holy Spirit and has an anointing on it to bear fruit or prosper. Many times, it's not the you're doing the wrong thing but since you're not submitting to Jesus, your efforts don't have an anointing (which is the supernatural enabling of God) to bear the results you need to happen in your life.

Think about it this way. Jesus was a carpenter by trade. But you can now flip through the phone book and find many carpenters. If you found the best carpenter out there and they constructed a building and Jesus using the same blue prints constructed the same building, which building would you want? Jesus' building would be the best building because during His time of carpentry, He was Anointed to be a carpenter meaning God specifically empowered Him to prosper as a carpenter so any building or project He worked on was completed as if God completed it Himself.

God is also saying you can manage your marriage but if you let me manage it, I'll manage it to perfection, I'll manage your money better than all the best minds of Wall Street and I'll manage your health better than the best medically educated doctors. When you submit to Jesus and follow His ways as the sheep follow the Shepherd, He'll led you to your identity and purpose which will bring fulfillment in every area of your life.

### 4. *Loves his life Loses it*

To help you make the decision of dying to self and submitting to God or not, Jesus gives us a contrast of what you can expect from your life based on the decision you make. Jesus says:

*He that loveth his life shall lose it; and he that hateth his life in this world shall keep it unto life eternal. – John 12:25*

Jesus says that the one who refuses to submit to Him and insist on doing things their own way will lose their life. Look at the problems you're facing right now in your life; you've been trying to make them better according to your own wisdom and way of doing things and look how those situations have not gotten better but in most instances, have gotten worst.

Jesus is saying you're slowly but surely losing your life.

- ➢ Divorce occurs when you try to do marriage your way instead of God's way.
- ➢ Debt occurs when you manage finances your way.
- ➢ Everything you try to do on your own fails and you're losing your life because you would rather do things your own way rather than submit to God.

You love your life too much to die so that Jesus may live through you.

### 5. Hate his Life
*He that hates his life shall keep it unto life eternal*

The person who acknowledges that their way is out of sync with God's way and submit to God will reap the benefits of a joyous life. He acknowledges the fact that God thinks on a higher level than me so I'm going to submit to His way of thinking even if I don't understand what He's doing right now. But because he's willing to die to himself; and separate who he *thinks* he is from who he *really* is so that Jesus can reign within him, he experiences victory after victory and blessing after blessing. Understand this, submitting to Jesus does not mean there will be no hardships in your life. It only means that during the storms, you will have peace that surpasses all understanding because you know that because you are submitted to God and following the Shepherd, the storm will not overtake you.

### 6. *Follow Jesus*

We have many people who say they believe in Jesus, but the question is are you following Him. To follow Jesus, you must first die to your own agenda.

### 7. *Where I am my Servant Will Be*

If you are following Jesus and are submitted to him, your actions should line up with His Word. That way you will be found where He is. You cannot say I'm following Jesus and continue to do things according to your own way because Jesus is not submitted to *your* way, you are supposed to be submitted in His.

### 8. *Father Honors*

To be honored is to be held in High Regard in front of others. When you die to yourself and submit to Jesus, God Honors and hold you in high regard in front of others and that's when people can begin to see and say God favors you.

Discovering your identity begins with discovering God and dying to self. When you make God the Lord of your life and die to your personal agenda, your own the path of discovering who you *really* are.

# Chapter 10

## DELIVER ME FROM MY ISSUES

*"Now a certain woman had a flow of blood for twelve years, and had suffered many things from many physicians. She had spent all that she had and was no better, but rather grew worse. When she heard about Jesus, she came behind Him in the crowd and touched His garment. For she said, 'If only I may touch His clothes, I shall be made well.'"*

– Mark 5:25-34

Looking at the above verses of scripture, we see a woman in a hopeless situation, desperately seeking to get into the presence of Jesus. This woman has been dealing with an issue of blood for twelve long years and has finally reached her breaking point to where she has made it up in her mind that *this* day *must* be the day that her condition is healed. In her desperation to get to Jesus, she is forced to fight her way through a crowd that is surrounding Him filled with people who are desperate to have their own infirmities remedied. Realizing that because of the crowd she probably will not be able to get to Jesus to share her struggles with him face to face, this hopeless woman; now down on her knees, steps out on faith and determines that if I can just touch the hem of His garment, I will be healed.

Upon stretching out her hand and grabbing hold of the hem of Jesus' robe, she felt within herself the fountain producing the flow of blood shut off. Amid her joy, she becomes afraid as she hears the source of her healing yell out, "Who touched Me!" This woman, with fear and trembling comes before Jesus, falls to her knees with her head bowed before Him and begins to pour out her struggles to Him. After pouring out all the ugly details of her pain and struggle to Jesus, He responds to her by saying your faith has made you whole.

## *Being Whole*

I want to share with you the significance of Jesus' statement of being made whole. To be *made* whole, you must first be lacking in some area. We are all lacking in some areas of our life. If we are depressed, we are lacking joy, if we are broke, we are lacking prosperity, if we are sick, we are lacking health. Being whole means that you are complete without any shortcomings in that area of your life.

When you get whole, it means that you have the fullness of God filling that area of your life. It's not enough to just be financially rich, but when you have the fulfilling of God in your finances, you are whole because you realize that God is the resource and not your money. When you have the fulfilling of God in your health, you realize that it's not the medicine that's making you healthy, but your health is complete because of the presence of God in your sick situation.

Everybody has their own struggles and issues that they are enduring and trying to overcome, and it is these very struggles that prevent us from being whole and living a complete life enjoying the fullness of Jesus Christ. In some shape, form or fashion, we all suffer from our own "*Issue of Blood*," and we need the presence of Jesus in our situation to dry up the fountain.

### *Saw Many Physicians*

The Bible says this woman saw many physicians and spent all that she had and still didn't get better; in fact, the Bible says she saw her situation get worse. I know that it didn't take this woman 12 years to begin searching for help. I believe that once her issue of blood began, she saw it as her regular bodily function. But once it didn't stop when it was supposed to stop, she probably immediately went to the doctor, only to hear, give it a few more days.

This lady went to her primary care physician, was referred to specialist after specialist. She had undergone all the experimental treatments and took every prescription and tried every home remedy, but nothing worked. She spent all that she had but didn't get better, her condition only got worse.

Just like this woman, when we get fed up with the situations in our life, we go looking for help. We seek the advice of others, read articles and try everything we can find that addresses our situation. But just like this woman, when we try to handle our situation and overcome our struggle, rather than making it better, we make it worse because we've reached a situation that we are not supposed to handle. And since we are not supposed to handle the situation, we cannot solve the problem on our own. When we are lacking in certain areas of our life and are not whole, we try all the tricks of the trade but none of them will work because only Jesus can make us whole.

The reason only Jesus can make us whole in these situations and only Jesus could make this woman whole is because the issue of blood this woman was forced to endure was not a physical illness as much as it were a spiritual illness. Her issue of blood was a spiritual illness designed by the enemy to separate and prevent this woman from having a relationship with God.

Not everything we go through is *just* a sickness, or *just* a financial hardship or *just* a struggle; but some issues are attacks from the enemy designed to prevent or destroy your relationship with Jesus.

## *Issue of Blood*

Whenever we hear this story, we think about the physical problems this woman had to endure as she struggled with her issue of blood. But the desperation that drove this woman to seek the healing power of Jesus was from more than just her physical condition. Because she had an issue of blood, this woman was ceremonially unclean according to scripture (*See Lev. 15:19*). Because she was ceremonially unclean, it meant that she was not able to go into the temple (Church), nor was she able to offer a sacrifice to God.

Because she was not able to enter the temple or offer a sacrifice to God, she was not able to go to the High Priest and ask him to intercede on her behalf and pray to God for her healing. The Jewish Law laid out several things that made you ceremonial unclean which prohibited you from entering the temple and worshipping God. The Law also gave strict instructions on purification and the length of time a person had to wait before they could resume their worshipping practices towards God.

The monthly menstruation of a woman according to Jewish law is what made a woman ceremonially unclean. The Law required a woman to separate herself from everyone else during this time because anyone or anything she touched became unclean. When a woman's menstruation ended, according to the law she still had to remain separated from everyone and everything for seven days before she would be considered clean.

The Law also stated that if the woman maintained an issue, she was unclean and must be separated. However, this woman's issue of blood was a continuous problem that was permanently prohibiting her from entering the presence of God. Being ceremonially unclean meant that she was cut off from God until her uncleanness ran its course.

Because she had an issue of blood which made her unclean, anyone she touched became unclean, so for 12 years, she had to be separated from her friends, her family, her church and her God. Not only did she have to deal with the daily discomfort of her condition, but she had to endure being ostracized from her community. No one wanted to be around her, everybody avoided her, and everyone was gossiping about her.

## *Our Issues*

We all have our own "*Issues*" we must endure. We've all had some situations we had to endure by ourselves because they were so ugly and so nasty that nobody else wanted to be around us, they didn't want to be seen associating with us but when they got around other folks, they talked about us like a dog. In the beginning, your feelings got hurt because you were embarrassed about your situation and you knew people talking about you. You saw people you used to call friend turn their back on you, people who were supposed to be family walk away from you. Then you got tired of having to deal with everything by yourself.

You get tired of worrying about with other people saying about you behind your back and now you start looking for help to overcome whatever you are going through. When we reach this stage, we reach desperation. This woman probably heard that there was a man from Nazareth who claimed to be the Son of God. She'd probably heard that He gave a blind man sight, a deaf man the ability to hear and on several occasions brought back to life those the doctors had officially pronounced to be dead.

She probably said within herself, I don't know if He's the Son of God or not, I don't know if He's the promised Messiah and I don't know if the healing miracles everybody talking about are true. All I know is that I've tried everything else. I've seen all the doctors and took all the medicine. What could it hurt for me to track this man down and try Him for myself?

When we get desperate enough and fed up enough with our situation, we'll aggressively seek an encounter with Jesus and we won't care who or how many people are in our way. This woman didn't care how many people stood between her and Jesus, she knew for her to get healed, she had to have an encounter with Him.

## *Flow Stopped Immediately*

As she fought her way through the crowd she realized, she would be able to get to Jesus. In her last act of desperation, she got down on her knees and stretched out her hand and touched the hem of His garment and the Bible says that the flow of blood stopped immediately.

When we meet Jesus, and place our situations at his feet, whatever we are lacking must be fulfilled; meaning the source of our problem must be *cut off* because the weapons designed to separate us from God cannot stand in the presence of God.

## ***Fear & Trembling***

Realizing that her struggle with this sickness was over, this woman experienced joy within her spirit but only for a short while. Just as soon as she was healed, she heard Jesus shout out, "Who touched Me!"

She knew at that moment that Jesus had the power and ability to heal, but she did not know what kind of person he was. Was He like the priest who forbid her to come into the church because she was unclean? Was He like the Pharisees who tried to live their life strictly abiding by the law and would be offended because she touched His clothing? Is He going to be mad because I touched Him?

She responded to Jesus in fear and trembling because in the midst of trying to get to Him through the crowd, she had to touch other people. Because she had an issue of blood and she was ceremonially unclean, by touching a countless number of people to get to Jesus, according to the Law, she had inadvertently made them unclean as well. Not only that, according to the Law, because she touched Jesus, she had just made him unclean too.

When we really examine ourselves, and see the filth covering us and realize how it separates us from God and how nobody else wants to be around us, we can easily develop the mindset that we are not able to be cleansed by God. But just as this woman's *"Issue"* was not enough to cause Jesus to become unclean and unworthy to intercede on her behalf with God, neither are any of our problems or issues filthy enough or beyond the redeeming ability of Jesus Christ to help us.

This woman came before Jesus and kneeled before Him at his feet with complete humility. And she poured out her pain before Him acknowledging that she did not have the ability to cleanse herself or heal herself.

But because she had faith to believe that He could, she was made whole. Our faith in Jesus' redeeming ability is what makes us whole and complete. When we believe that Jesus can bring the presence of God into every situation of our life, Jesus will bring the presence of God into every situation of our life. And having the presence of God in every situation of our life is essential to us not only discovering our identity in Him but living out that identity.

# Chapter 11

## LEAVING THE KNOWN FOR THE UNKNOWN

*"The Lord had said to Abram, 'Go from your country, your people and your father's household to the land I will show you.'"*
— Genesis 12:1

In the above verse of scripture, God tells Abram who would become known as Abraham to leave his family, leave his home; leave everything he has ever known behind to go to a place that God would show him. God told Abraham to go to an unknown place, but God named specific blessings Abraham would receive for being obedient. God told him that He would make Abraham a great nation, that He would bless him and make his name great so that Abraham would be a blessing. God also told Abraham that He would bless those who bless him and curse those who curse him and that through him, all the families of the earth shall be blessed.

    As Christians, we will often be told by God to leave behind our most comfortable and familiar environments for the uncomfortable and unknown. To discover our identity in God, we must leave behind the familiarly false identities we've created for ourselves. For being obedient to the will and command of God, we will receive blessings that are unimaginable to us because we will experience true fulfillment in our lives once we know our identity. When we know our identity, we can operate in our purpose and experience life in way we never thought possible. God will take us places and allow us to experience opportunities that we never conceived in our mind.

However, if we are willing to be honest with ourselves, many times throughout our lives, we miss out on experiencing the blessings of God because we will not leave our comfortable environment for the *unknown* and *uncomfortable* because we are content in our safe and familiar surroundings of life. Although we may not be completely happy or satisfied with our lives, we've become content in the familiarity of life and the identity that we've always known. Our flesh or natural mind rejects and rebels against the will and direction of God for our lives and we rationalize our rebellion by saying that we are just using good common sense when what we are doing is refusing to step out on faith like Abraham.

For example, let's say you have a fantastic job. You love your job; it pays well, you have good benefits, you like the people and there just isn't much bad you could think of or say about your job. Then one day you hear the voice of God say, "Quit your job and I'll guide you to the land of freedom and prosperity." Many of us would say "No, that's crazy! I can see if I had something better lined up but to just up and quit, that's stupid." See, we rationalize not stepping out on faith to walk out into the land of the *unknown* and *uncomfortable* that God is trying to direct us to as using good common sense.

We ask God questions like, "How am I going to feed my family, pay my bills, pay the car note." We have an endless list of why we cannot do what God is calling us to do just like Moses telling God all the reasons he cannot go to Egypt as God's deliverer. Leaving what we know and what we're comfortable with is a shock to our natural mind. But we are to be spiritually minded, walking by faith and not by sight (*See 2 Cor. 5:7*). When we walk by faith we are walking by what we know God told us to do and not what we see or think with our natural mind.

You may be saying right now, "I want to step out on faith and trust God and walk out into the unknown and uncomfortable to a place that God will show me. But I don't know how to step out in faith like that."

There are two things that I want to share with you that will help empower you to leave the comfortable for the uncomfortable and the known for the unknown with full confidence.

## *Establish A Growing Relationship with God*

To develop the confidence to step out on faith and leave the known and comfortable for the unknown and uncomfortable, the first thing we must do is establish a relationship with God if we haven't done so already. For any of the blessings and favor of God to be present and activated in your life, you must first confess Jesus as your personal Lord and Savior.

After making God the head of your life, the second thing you should do is grow your relationship with God. Studying the Word of God regularly, prayer and meditation are how we develop a growing relationship with God. This is where we get our confidence in God and can hear and discern the voice of God. Prayer and Meditation are two of the most neglected spiritual disciplines but are also two of the most important. Prayer is more than just saying our grace before we eat or saying our prayers before we go to sleep at night.

Prayer is a conversation with God, so we should pray continuously throughout our day. We draw strength from God when we pray. When we pray, we are spending time with God. The more time we spend with God in prayer, the more intimate we get with God and the more we grow closer to God. We should make it a habit to pray often.

Meditation is also important in growing more intimate and closer to God. Meditation goes hand in hand with the Word of God and our personal study. Meditation is reflecting on God's word or a situation or issue in relation to the Word of God or simply reflecting on God Himself. This is where a lot of people begin to hear God's voice more clearly. You become wrapped in God's glory and His presence and you begin to get more intimate with Him.

In this stage of intimacy, we begin to become empowered by God as we reflect on and gain a revelation of the magnitude of promises. And we begin to gain an understanding of our purpose as God begins to give us revelation of our identity through the Word of God.

Prayer and meditation is where our relationship with God must begin for us to develop a level of trust and confidence in Him. It is through prayer and meditation that God will lay out His plan for you so that when He tells you to leave the *known* for the *unknown* and the *comfortable* for the *uncomfortable* you'll have the confidence that you will arrive at the destination God has spoken or shown to you when everything else around you point to the contrary.

It was because he spent time with God that Moses developed the confidence to walk into the Egyptian palace with a stick and tell Pharaoh the most powerful man on the face of the Earth at that time that God seen said let His people go. It was because Noah had spent time with God that he was able to go out a build the Ark. Here was Noah in the middle of the dessert, with water anywhere to be seen building a boat. People thought he was crazy.

## IDENTITY

When we step out of the known into the unknown, people are going to talk about us. They are going to call us crazy. But they haven't seen the vision that God has shown us, nor the voice of God speak to us. We know what we're walking towards, and even though we cannot see it, because God said it we believe Him.

# Chapter 12

## STRETCHED TO THE NEXT LEVEL

*"I will make you a great nation; I will bless you and make your name great; and you shall be a blessing."*

– Genesis 12:1

Many times, in our lives, God is calling us away from the known and the comfortable just like He did with Abram. However, rather than stepping out into the unknown, we try to hold on to the things God wants us to release. When we look at God's call to Abram, He tells him to leave his country. What God is telling Abram to do is leave the place you know as home and get away from the comforts of familiar surroundings. If we stay in comfortable familiar surroundings, we limit ourselves from the possibility of stepping into the place of unexpected blessings. Familiar surroundings are just that, familiar and predictable. Nothing new happens in familiar surroundings. If something new happened, it wouldn't be considered familiar. It is familiarity that makes it comfortable. However, if we are consumed with predictability, we are not able to receive anything new and unexpected from God.

When we live our lives knowing exactly what the day has in store for us, our mindset begins to limit us to expecting to have the same experiences as yesterday. Since we are stuck in yesterday, we are not receptive of a *today* move from God. God operates in the unexpected and the only way to experience God in a new way is to get out of the comforts of the expected and into the uncomfortableness of the unexpected. So, the first thing God tells Abram to do is get away from familiar surroundings. God is saying, if I can get you to change your scenery so that you can begin to see something new daily, you'll develop an expectation of having unexpected experiences daily. Once God can get you to begin expecting the unexpected by changing your scenery, He can give you a new vision for your life.

If there are places in our life that have become familiar and predictable, we need to begin listening for God to tell us to move. If we remain in predictable situations in our life, we cannot expect God to show up with unexpected blessings. God cannot do the unexpected in your life in a place where your mindset has limited you to expect the routine.

The next thing God told Abram to do in the above scripture was get away from his family. God not only wants Abram to separate himself from the familiarity of his surroundings, but He also wants him to separate himself from the familiarity of the people that's around him. We must realize that there are people in our lives who are not doing anything with their life. Although in some cases they may be doing something with their life, they are not moving in the same direction that God is trying to move us.

When we have a desire to go to another level we must understand that to get there, rather than surrounding ourselves with people who continuously operate on the same level of predictability, we must begin surrounding ourselves with people who are striving to go higher as well as those who are already operating on a higher level.

If we remain around the same people engaging in the same activities, having the same conversations, our minds are never challenged to explore new possibilities. Just as God uses us to be a blessing and an influence in the lives of others, He will use other people to be a blessing and an influence in our lives. However, if are mindsets are limited to the predictable familiarity of the people around us, we are not able to receive anything new from them because we don't have a level of expectation to receive anything new from them.

God wants us to begin surrounding ourselves with new people who are doing the things He's leading us to do as well as surround ourselves with others who are striving in our direction. It's when we get away from the comforts of the familiarity of the people around us into the uncomfortable and unexpectedness of new people that we develop a mindset to expect something from them that we've never experienced before.

Once our mindset begins to expect new experiences from new people, God can begin blessing us with unexpected blessings from unexpected people. But it all starts with us getting out of our comfort zones, getting away from familiarity and allowing God to direct our paths to unfamiliar places and new people.

# Chapter 13

## WHERE IS YOUR VISION

*"Where there is no vision, the people perish: but he that keeps the law, happy is he"*

- Proverbs 29:18

Are you just floating through life with no vision of the destiny you're trying to reach? Is there even a vision of destiny for you to pursue in the first place? When you have no vision, you live a life of hopelessness because you have nothing to look forward to; you have no driving force motivating you or propelling you into your destiny or the next dimension of your life.

The writer of this Proverbs says, "Where there is no vision, the people perish..." To perish means to die or have an untimely demise.

When you have no vision of where you're going, you often end up on the wrong road to nowhere because you don't have a map or a game plan to guide your actions in life. When you have no vision for your life, you have a temporary outlook of life. To have a temporary outlook on life means you place more stock; or more value on *right now* rather than taking into consideration anything that deals with your future.

Many people with no vision of where they are going have ruined their destiny by being caught up and concerned with what's going on right now.

We as a nation and we as a body of believers have lost our vision. We've lost our vision for our future and have settled into chasing temporary fulfillment rather than everlasting peace. Because we as a body of believers have lost our vision, we seldom conqueror unfamiliar territory or going to new dimensions in our lives.

We go to our charismatic churches and shout about *"changing the atmosphere,"* and talk about *"going to the next level"* with other Christians because it has become a part of our "religious lingo." But the truth of the matter is we are not expanding our territory because we don't have a vision within ourselves to do so.

The Bible says that we are to raise up a child in the way that they should go so that when they get old, they will not depart from it (*See Prov. 22:6*). However, when you have a generation of God's people with no vision for their own life and are never in the position to prosper or go to the next dimension in any area of their life, they have nothing to point to showing the next generation that by writing the vision and leaning on God to bring it to manifestation we can change the circumstances of our lives. Because of that, we have a generation of young people with no vision for their life, so they take no personal pride in the way they carry themselves within society.

When we have a generation of young people putting tattoos across their face, neck and body, we're looking at a generation of people who are focused on the temporary rather than the future, because they have no vision and no knowledge of their identity in God. The reason their lives have descended into such chaos is because we as a Body of Believers did not have a vision for ourselves and were not adequately able to impart a vision into the lives of the next generation.

Where there is no vision, the people perish. We the people bring an untimely demise to our destiny because we are focused on fulfilling the present rather than establishing the future; and because we never reach our place of destiny to fulfill our purpose and contribute to our community it brings an untimely demise to our society as well. You man of God, you woman of God have a purpose in your life, something to contribute to the world that helps expand the Kingdom of God but where is your vision?

A man with no vision is a dangerous man because he has nothing to lose. He's like a wild animal looking for something to devour just to feel a sense of purpose. Not realizing that birthing a vision in your spirit will change your whole reality and give you purpose in life. A woman without vision is a woman without values. She doesn't know her worth so she gives herself away cheap because she has no vision of seeing herself as the queen God has called and created her to be.

Not only must we have a vision for our own lives to propel and motivate us into our destiny, but we must bring our children up in the way that they should go so that when they get older, rather than taking the wrong roads to nowhere, they'll hold true to declaring and decreeing a vision for their lives. When we have no vision, we are dead on the inside; meaning all possibility of hope for better or different has been exhausted or eliminated from the thought of ever being possible.

You must have a vision for everything you do.

- If you are cooking breakfast, there should be a vision of what the outcome of the meal is going to look like.

- If you are going to work, there should be a vision for the progression of your career.
- If you are having children, there should be a vision for the home life you want to bring that child up in and there should be a vision for the future prospect for that child so that when He or She grows up, they can inherit a vision for their life instead of roaming hopelessly through life because nothing has been imparted into them.

There must be a vision for everything you do. What is your vision for the day, for the week, for the month, for the year, the next five years of your life? Your vision helps establish a plan of action to propel you into your future; your destiny. Where there is no vision, the people perish.

- Do you feel bored in your life? It might be that you lack vision which will add excitement to your life.

- Do you feel you're spinning your wheels in whatever you're doing? It might be that you lack vision that will give you clear direction.

- Are your children raising more hell than a little bit; constantly getting into trouble? It might be that you have not imparted a vision into their lives that inspires them to move beyond the temporary and embrace the eternal.

The time for waiting on God to move is over. God is waiting on you to write the vision and make it plain. Let it be your guiding and motivating force to make changes in your life, changes in your children, changes in your finances, changes in every area of your life so that we can make Godly changes in the world.

# Chapter 14

## CALL FORTH YOUR POTENTIAL

*"Now it came to pass after these things that God tested Abraham, and said to him, 'Abraham!' And he said, 'Here I am.' Then He said, 'Take now your son, your only son Isaac, whom you love, and go to the land of Moriah, and offer him there as a burnt offering on one of the mountains of which I shall tell you.'"*
– Genesis 22:1-2

God created all of us with a purpose in mind. He endowed all of us with the potential we need to function in and accomplish the purpose for our lives. However, for us to operate in our purpose, we must call forth our potential. Potential is the capacity to become or develop into something in the future that leads to success. To fulfill your purpose, you must first call forth your potential.

God prepares us for our purpose by helping us to call forth our potential. Calling forth our potential means that our lives must first be put in divine order which means God must transition your life from chaos to order. Looking at the text, Abraham goes on to be known throughout the Bible as the Father of Faith. Now, it truly can be said that there were times in the beginning of their relationship where Abraham did not fully trust God. It can be said that there were times early on in their relationship that Abraham placed other things; things he thought we more important to himself ahead of God.

Now, it was during these times of their early relationship that God still had a purpose for Abraham's life but Abraham was not yet operating in his purpose because he had not yet realized his full potential in God. We must develop the mindset and desire to be fully engulfed in God. It is only when we are fully engulfed in God that we can realize our full potential in God. When we recognize our full potential in God, God can begin using us to operate in our purpose.

Our purpose is the thing that God created us for; created us to do and potential is the capacity to develop into something that leads to future success. God cannot place you on the path of purpose if you don't yet have the potential to be successful. To prepare you for purpose, God must first call forth your potential by putting your life in divine order. If you look at your life and your relationship with God right now and compare it to Abraham's relationship with God in its beginning stages, you are certain to see some similarities. Similarities such as times where we just don't trust God fully with certain things in your lives.

There are things that we place a higher value on and priority in over God whether we realize it or not. We can say that we don't place or value anything else above God but the proof is not in your words but in your everyday actions. Many times, we face struggles in our life because God is trying to bring our life into divine order. Divine Order means that God's priorities become our priorities. Whatever I think or thought was important takes a back seat to make room for what God says is important.

Divine Order means it doesn't matter what I think is right it doesn't matter what's popular in society, I live my life according to God's principles not because I believe it's right but because it *is* right. We get so full of ourselves now a day's saying I don't agree with that, I don't think that's right or times have changed...

None of what we say or believe matters because our opinion has no place in God's decision making. The first thing God does to call forth our potential is to bring our lives from chaos to order by establishing divine order in our lives.

The more Abraham walked with God, talked with God, worshiped God, and praised God, the more he began to trust God. Again, we must get pass the mindset of that's good enough in our relationship with God. Abraham didn't just submit some areas of his life to God; he submitted every area of his life to God. Because Abraham submitted every area of his life to God, he could faithfully trust God with every area of his life.

We place ourselves on a spiritual roller coaster by picking and choosing which areas of our lives we will let God handle and which areas we will handle ourselves. We may trust God to keep us safe in traffic but trust ourselves when it comes to our finances. Once we find ourselves in a situation where we have done all that we can do on our own in the areas we have kept away from God, we try to bring Him in at the last minute. Our emotions rise and fall wondering if God's going to come through for us because we have not established a relationship of trust with Him in that area of our life. We rob ourselves from having a peaceful life.

## *Establishing Trust*

As Abraham begins to trust God more, the Bible says that God tested Abraham. He told him to take his son Isaac, the son of the covenant that was promised to him and sacrifice him on the altar as a burnt offering. God tested the motives and heart of Abraham to see if they were pure and genuine towards God.

Occasionally, God tests all of us to see if our heart and motives for our relationship with Him is sincere and true. There's nothing like getting into a sticky situation and the one you thought had your back turns and runs for the hills leaving you hanging. That's why an untested faith cannot be trusted. When God puts you on the path of your purpose, He needs to know that you're willing to have His back when everything is speaking against and fighting against the purpose for which He created you.

Your purpose is not about you, it's about God using you to usher in a new dimension or strengthening an established part of His kingdom to accomplish His divine purposes. God tested Abraham; telling Him to make Isaac a burnt offering. God still does the same thing with us today; it's just not an actual burnt offering. The burnt offering is symbolic of the total consecration of the worshiper to God.

Because the offering is completely consumed and no part is left for human consumption, the burnt offering symbolized a sacrificing of self.

When we consecrate ourselves to God, nothing of our own self is to be allowed to remain or have its own way over God's way. For any of our self to remain means hindrance for us fulfilling God's purpose for our lives remains.

The parts of the burnt offering sacrifice are the wood, the offering and the fire. The wood was used to build the altar. The wood symbolized every area of personal desire in our lives. Our desires had to be laid down to make way for God's use of our lives. Every selfish desire would be replaced with God's desire.

The offering that was laid on the wooden altar symbolizes *you*. You are fully and willingly laying down your life for God's use and His purposes. The Fire represents God. God is a consuming fire which means as the sacrifice and the altar are burned up, it signified that God wanted *all* of you for Himself...Not just part.

God required the burnt offering twice a day every day. To know your identity and live a life of boundless joy, great peace and great happiness, you must lay your life day for God daily throughout the day so that you can live a life of purpose.

God promised Abraham a son through his wife Sarah that would serve as his heir. Now God puts Abraham to the test. God says lay down your desires and offer up to me the one thing I gave you as a promise to fulfill the covenant we've made; which is your son Isaac. Abraham willingly prepares Isaac as a burnt offering sacrifice because he has moved passed just trusting God in certain areas and at certain times. He now trusts God in *all* things.

Since Abraham trusts God in all things now, he's not moved by what the situation looks like. He's resting in the promise of God and the ability of God. Because Abraham was willing to sacrifice his son as requested by God, he can recognize within himself that he is fully engulfed in God. Because Abraham is fully engulfed in God, he is ready to operate at his full potential in God which makes him ready to live out the purpose God has for his life.

To call forth your potential, you must allow God to put your life in Divine Order.

# Chapter 15

## SUCCESS EMBEDDED WITHIN US

*"Then God said, 'Let the earth bring forth grass, the herb that yields seed, and the fruit tree that yields fruit according to its kind, whose seed is, on the earth'; and it was so."*

— Genesis 1:11-12

In the beginning during the creationary process, God created all the vegetation of the Earth. He created the trees, the fruit and the vegetables. As He created these things, He didn't create them to be purposeless. He created them with a perpetual purpose. Perpetual purpose means that if they have life within them, they can produce and be productive. God did this by creating seed bearing vegetation with the ability to produce or reproduce after its own likeness.

If you cut open an apple there are seeds in it. If you cut open an orange, there are seeds in it and if you cut open a cucumber there are seeds in it. If you plant those seeds, they will produce the very thing they came from. Jeremiah the prophet said before I was formed in my mother's womb, before the foundations of the Earth were formed, you knew me and ordained me to preach to the nations *(See Jer. 1:5)*. Jeremiah is saying that before God created any of us, not only did He create us with a purpose, but He placed within us the ability to be successful in our purpose. Before God spoke any of creation into existence, He gave us an identity.

## *Success in our Purpose*

When we look at Matthew, we see a man has turned over his possessions to three of his servants. To one he gave five talents. To another he gave two talents and to the last he gave one talent (*See Matt. 25:14-18*). There are five things about being successful in fulfilling our purpose as well as in our life that we can take away from the text in Matthew.

## *We're Not all Equal*

The first thing we must understand when it comes to being successful is that none of us are equal; none of us have the same ability. There are some things you do better than most other people around you and there are some things that they do that are better than you. You can practice it and work hard at trying to perfect it. You can study it for years while they do nothing and they will still have a greater ability to do that thing that they are good at better than you because they are gifted with the ability to do it.

We often hinder our ability to call forth our potential because we're working so hard to be like someone else and do what somebody else is doing. We focus so much on what we're not gifted by God to do that we fail to see the potential in what we are gifted by God to do. The potential that resides in you is a gift from God that will enable and empower you to be successful in doing what God has called you to do. Whatever gift God has given you, He has given you the ability to reproduce the quality of its value from within your spirit to a physical manifestation of something great for His purpose, all of which is tied into your identity.

David played the harp. David played the harp to entertain himself while he was out in the pasture by himself tending to his father's sheep. Now, anybody

# IDENTITY

could play the harp and there were probably many talented harp players during this time but none of them were gifted like David. Because David was a gifted harp player, it was only his harp playing that would sooth King Saul whenever the spirit would come and torment Him (*See 1 Sam. 16:23*).

Although David was a gifted musician, not just anybody could go in to see the king. There is a certain way you had to present yourself, conduct yourself and dress yourself while you were in the presence of the king. David had to learn all these things before he could play his harp for King Saul. Being in the presence of King Saul, David no doubt heard the daily affairs of the king's business discussed as well as the decisions the king had to make daily.

When David became King, he knew how to conduct himself as a king all because he called forth his potential as a gifted harp player. David's musical gift reproduced the quality of its value by establishing the eternal throne for which Jesus will sit on and reign. No matter how much they tried, no other harp player could do what David did because David had a God-given gift. Similarly, no one else can do what you can do with your God-given gift because it is ordained and established by God.

Your gift is not to keep you where you are but to open the doors to where God wants you to be. Since God has a different place He wants all of us to be, we are not all created equally to do the same things. We don't all have the same ability. You must find your gift and call forth your own potential to get where God wants you to be.

## ***Success is a product of our Effort***

Many times, whether we believe it or not, we think that if God has a purpose for us; an assignment for us, while living we will inevitably fulfill that purpose or assignment. But I submit to you that fulfilling your purpose must be intentional. Success in the things of God must be intentional, which means we must put intentional action or intentional work towards our purpose to be successful. Success in our purpose, fulfilling our God given purpose is a product of effort.

In the text (*See Matt. 25:14-18*), when the master left, the bible says that immediately the man with the five talents and the man with the two talents went to work. The man with the five talents earned five additional talents and the man with two talents earned two additional talents. They both could reproduce the value of the talents they were given because again, whatever gift God has given you, He has given you the ability to reproduce the quality of its value.

The master represents God; the servants represent the people of God. God gave one servant five talents. If God gave him five talents as a gift to use, it means that God has placed within him the ability to reproduce the quality of the gifts value that was given to Him. This man used his gift and prospered in the assignment given to him by his master because he knew the potential that was within himself.

The same can be said for the servant with the two talents. He knew his potential; he called forth that potential and became successful in the assignment given to him by the master. These two men did not wait for the master to give them step by step instructions on what to do with the gift given to them.

Each of them in their own way put their gift to work like only they could.

We must get off the sidelines waiting for God to put us in the game, we need to realize that we're already in the game and start playing. We sit waiting for God to open doors and spell everything out for us, but God opens doors of success when we're moving towards success. He cannot open anything while we're sitting still.

What's your purpose in life? Are you working towards it? How are you working towards it? What gifts has God giving you that you are or are not using?

## **_God gives us what we need to fulfill our Purpose_**

When we look at nature, God didn't just make the fruit and vegetables and tell them to figure out a way to reproduce themselves. He placed seed within them to reproduce after their kind. He gave them everything they needed to reproduce after their own likeness.

In the text (*See Matt. 25:14-18*), when the master left, he didn't just tell the servants to go make him more money. What he did was give them something to use in conjunction with the gift that already resided within them. He gave them everything they needed to fulfill their purpose.

In the same manner, God has a purpose for your life and He has embedded potential within you that will empower you to be successful in fulfilling that purpose. He didn't say go spread the Kingdom and not give us what we needed to do just that. Everything you need to be successful in the things of God, the purpose for which He created you resides within you. You must call forth your potential. You must get a revelation of what you can do in the name of Jesus and the power of His might.

## ***We work for the Master Not Ourselves***

I believe most of the time, the things that God wants us to do are the things we don't want to do. Because we have fooled ourselves into believing that we work for ourselves and provide our own needs and are living life for ourselves, we're not doing most of the things God wants us to be doing in our life. We must understand the significance of the scripture that tells us we are not our own because we were bought with a price (*See 1 Corinthians 6:19-20*). Since you don't belong to yourself, you not a free man, you not a free woman, you are a slave to the one who purchased you.

We are slaves to Jesus who bought us with His blood. And since we are slaves, every breath we take is to please the master. Everything we do in life is about working in the master's vineyard to prepare His harvest.

- What about my needs? You are a slave; the master will provide for your needs (*See Phil 4:19*).
- What about my wants and desires? If you delight yourself in the master and His work, He will give you the desires of your heart (*See Psalm 37:4*).
- What if I don't want to do the masters work? You need to find a cross and go die for your own sins and then hope it's enough to purchase your freedom. But I can yell you now, it's not enough (*See Rom. 2:8-9*).

Your life is not your own. You can be successful according to the world's standards, but because you didn't fulfill the purpose God had for your life, you'll still be and feel like a failure. You work for the Master, not yourself.

## ***We Will be held Accountable***

When the Master gives us an assignment, we will be held accountable on whether we are successful in completing that assignment. When we look at the text in Matthew, we see that the master gives his possessions to three of his servants. He gave one servant five talents, He gave one servant two talents and he gave the third servant one talent.

The servant with five talents produced five more talents. The servant with two produced two more talents. But the servant who was given one talent took what was given to him and buried it in a hole in the ground.

Now, to get some understanding of exactly what we're talking about here, let's put this word *talent* into perspective. During this time of history, one talent was equal to 6,000 denarii. One denarii were worth one day's pay and could buy 10 Donkeys.

One denarii would equal about $20 dollars today. The servant with five talents had about $600,000.

($20 x 6000 denarii = $120,000. $120,000 x 5 talents = $600,000)

The servant with two talents had about $240,000. The servant with one talent had about $120,000. He took $120,000 and buried it in the ground. The bible tells us that the master gave each servant talents based on their own ability. Which means that if the master gave this servant one talent or $120,000, it was because that servant at least had the ability to take that gift and produce out of it a value equal to what was given to him.

Rather than use the gift the master gave him; the servant hid his gift and did not prosper at all. When the master returned, he became angry with that servant and told him the least he could have done was put the money in the bank. He said if you had put the money in the bank it would have drew interest. Money generates money.

If your gift is playing the piano and you don't want to play the piano professionally, you shouldn't stop playing the piano, at least let the gift operate and do what it does. If you're an artist and don't want to be a professional artist, don't stop painting, the least you can do is operate in the gift at some capacity. At least people would have enjoyed listening to the music you played whether you got paid from it or not. At least people would have enjoyed looking at your paintings whether you sold them or not.

What gift has God given you? What assignment has he given you? Are you using your gift to complete your assignment? One day the master will return. On that day, the master will determine if you used what He gave you to fulfill your purpose or if you took your talent and hid it. Call forth your potential. Everything you need to be successful is embedded within you.

# Chapter 16

## DISCOVERING YOUR IDENTITY

*"Therefore, if anyone is in Christ, he is a new creation; old things have passed away; behold all things have become new."*

— 2 Corinthians 5:17

It is common for us to make plans for our lives. We have goals that we are pursuing and personal agendas that we've set for ourselves to accomplish in life. Many of us have an internal desire that when we've lived our life to completion, we want to be able to look back and say I did everything that I wanted to do and have no regrets because I didn't allow myself to miss out on anything. Now, it's prudent to make plans for your life, but we must be sensitive to what God desires to do with our lives and when He speaks, we must make His plans our priority. When we make God's plans for our life the priority, in some cases it will cause us to miss out on some of the things we really desired to do or were looking forward to accomplishing.

However, we must remember the fact that once we submit our lives to Jesus, we are bought with a price and have been made His. We belong to God and are now slaves of Jesus and our life is at His disposal to do with as He pleases. That's a difficult reality for some people to accept. But if you willingly submit your life to Christ and follow the path that He has for you, you will experience far greater joy and fulfillment in life than you could have ever imagined on the path you designed for yourself.

Many people desire to be wealthy in life, but for the purposes of God, they may never be. Many may want to travel the world, but God's desire and assignment for their life may require staying positioned in one region for the rest of their lives. Some may desire to work a simple 9-5 job without the headache of overwhelming responsibility. But for the glory of God's purposes, they may continuously advance to the highest levels of their profession so that they are in a position of influence to be used by God.

The key thing we must understand that will help us enjoy our life no matter what our situations may be; is understanding that our life belongs to God for Him to do with as He pleases. We must submit to Him and put our agenda on the back burner making His agenda our primary focus.

When we live our life flowing with God's program rather than fighting against His will for our life, we will get enjoyment in our life no matter what we face or what sacrifices we must make. We will get enjoyment in life because as we live our lives fulfilling the purpose God desires for us rather than fighting to achieve something He never for us, we live a life of pleasure in His presence.

We must understand that whatever pursuits of life we have are us attempting to create a false identity if it is not in line with the will of God and His purpose for our lives. God's sole purpose is to advance His Kingdom through the ministry of Jesus Christ which is at work within us and flows from us. For us to be used effectively for God's purposes we must come to the same realization as the song writer who said, *"My life is now my own, to Him I belong...,"* and we must willingly give ourselves to Him for the fulfillment of His purposes, then we will know our identity!

## ABOUT THE AUTHOR

Darrius Geter is the founder and senior pastor of Full Impact Christian Church in Snellville, Georgia and founder of The Full Impact Foundation. Geter is also the author of the life changing book *Violent Faith: It's Time to Get Violent!* Darrius and his wife Dayvener make their home in Monroe, Georgia with their four daughters.

Made in United States
Orlando, FL
01 November 2023